# academic
# writing

. . .

**jeanne godfrey**

palgrave

**Blackwell's/Palgrave Study Guides**

**Pocket Study Skills**

For a complete listing of all **Palgrave Study Skills** titles, please visit:
www.palgrave.com/studyskills

# contents

# introduction

A successful piece of academic writing communicates with its reader clearly and persuasively. It has high-quality content, a logical structure, a precise style and uses particular conventions to show how source material has been used. So, what does good academic writing look like and how can you make your own academic writing successful? This mini-guide will answer both of these questions.

Many of the tips in this guide are developed in the *Palgrave Study Skills* and *Pocket Study Skills* series, so these may be your next step for more detailed advice. Specific links are suggested at the bottom of the relevant pages throughout this guide.

# an example of student writing

On the next page are the first two paragraphs from an excellent 2,000-word essay, followed by the first two entries in the essay's list of references. The paragraphs have side-columns that comment on key features of language, style, content and structure. Other common forms of academic writing and assignments also need most of the features exemplified in the extract.

**Assignment title:** *Is the UK prison system effective?*

| Language and style | | Content and structure |
|---|---|---|
| Clear sentence structure that is formal but not too long or complicated.<br><br>Repetitions of key words or similar words (*prisons, prisons system, reoffend, ex-offender, crime, criminals*) that help focus and 'glue' the paragraphs together.<br><br>Words that are formal (although not overly so) and therefore precise and powerful (*deterrent, effective, achieving*). | Removing criminals from mainstream society is one of the two key objectives of prisons, the second being that a prison sentence should act as a deterrent to offending and reoffending. I will argue that the UK prison system is not effective in acting as a deterrent to reoffending, and that this high rate of reoffence in turn means that criminal activity is not being effectively reduced in the wider society. My proposition is, therefore, that the current UK prison system is not effective in achieving either of its two key goals.<br><br>In 2014, 46% of all adults released from UK prisons reoffended within a year, and this figure was even higher (58%) for adults who had finished a prison sentence of twelve months or less.[1] | First sentence introduces the topic succinctly and gives key points of definition and information.<br><br>The student then outlines the steps in their argument. They summarise their analysis of how things connect and the implications of these connections, leading to the proposition that addresses the essay title. |

| (Language and style) | | (Content and structure) |
|---|---|---|
| No use of emotional or subjective language, clichés or slang.<br><br>Use of words such as *this* and *these* which show how the sentences link. | The numbers are higher still for juveniles – nearly 70% of under-eighteens reoffended after release.[2] Moreover, these figures only show the number of ex-offenders who were actually caught committing crimes, and so the total percentage of ex-offenders involved in criminal activity in society is almost certainly higher. | The student summarises the supporting evidence and uses numbers (1, 2) to indicate where this information comes from. |
| | … | |
| *Ibid.* is a Latin abbreviation that means 'the same place as just mentioned' and indicates that source 2 is the same as source 1. | **List of references**<br>1  Prison Reform Trust (2014) *Prison: the facts. Bromley Briefing Summer 2014* p1.<br>http://www.prisonreformtrust.org.uk/Portals/0/Documents/Prison%20the%20facts%20May%202014.pdf *[Accessed on 1/3/2015]*<br>2  Ibid. | This style of reference list gives details of the sources in the order they were used in the essay. |

# writing critically

Academic study entails analysing things in detail, (breaking down and examining concepts and ideas) evaluating (finding weaknesses *and* strengths) and then from this analysis and evaluation, arriving at conclusions, solutions and knowledge creation.

One common reason students get low marks is that their writing contains too much non-critical content. Below are essay extracts that show you the difference between non-critical and critical writing.

---

### Non-critical writing

**Description**

Descriptive writing gives the *what* or *how* of something but does **not** give reasons, does not evaluate and does not try to persuade the reader of anything.

Example:

*The causes of ageism were first suggested by Butler (1969): a lack of understanding of older people, combined with fears about becoming old and a consequent desire for distance from old people.*

## Explanation

This can look like critical writing because it gives reasons and perhaps a conclusion, but explanation is still just stating fact. An explanation does **not** evaluate, argue or try to persuade.

Example:

> *Perdue and Gurtman (1990) concluded that due to the above factors, people developed unconscious negative associations with old age, thereby strengthening conscious negative attitudes and behaviours towards old people.*

## Opinion, agreement and disagreement

Opinion, agreement and disagreement are not aspects of critical writing, but points of view given without supporting evidence or logical reasoning. Opinion and dis/agreement are not valid arguments and in an academic text should only be given in addition to a properly supported argument, not instead of one.

## Critical writing

### Analysis

You will do much of your analysing in your head before you put it down in your writing. Analysing involves taking apart a statement, concept or argument in order to examine and define it in detail.

Example:

> *In their model, Perdue and Gurtman are talking about negative mental associations, but this is not the same as actual negative behaviour towards old people.*

### Evaluation

This involves weighing up the evidence and/ or argument, and deciding on its validity, value, relevance and implications.

Example:

*A weakness in their argument is the claim that negative associations are unconsciously learnt at an early age, because this has not in fact been proven.*

**Argument**

An argument is the whole sequence of initial claim (also called a proposition), supporting reasons and conclusion. The function of an argument is usually to try and persuade an audience of the validity of the proposition. An argument often takes a whole piece of writing to develop – below are just the concluding sentences of one.

Example:

*Although the extent of unconscious negative associations with older people can be debated, the evidence discussed here shows that they do exist. These associations are harder to address and redress than conscious prejudice, and this makes them a disproportionately damaging aspect of ageism in our society.*

For more on critical thinking and critical writing, see *Critical thinking skills*, *Getting critical* and *Writing for university*.

**3**

# using quotations

A quotation is a phrase or sentence/s taken from a source without any word changes. Good uses for quotations are:

- to state a fact or idea which the author has expressed in a unique and powerful way
- to establish or summarise an author's argument or position
- to provide an interesting/important start or end to your piece of writing
- to give the reader an original extract you then discuss in more detail.

## A quotation checklist

### 1 Is the quotation relevant to your point?

the student's point

**✗** Example:

*The main benefit of organ transplant is that it saves lives. As stated by Smith (2005), 'heart transplantation can save lives, but the procedure carries serious risks and complications and a high mortality rate' (p12).*

does not fully support the student's point

## 2   Have you introduced and/or commented on the quotation to show how it supports your point?

This sentence gives the student's point and introduces the supporting quotation

✔ Example:

*My main argument is that ethical behaviour is crucial to long-term business success and that, as Collins shows, 'good ethics is synonymous with good management' (Collins, 1994 p2). There are many examples of such success, including*

*...*

the student goes on to give examples that support their point and illustrate the quotation

## 3   Is the quotation worth quoting?

✘ Example:

*According to the Prison Reform Trust (2014) '46% of adults were reconvicted within one year of release.'*

This quotation gives a simple statistic and is not special enough to quote – the student should have paraphrased this information, i.e. put it into their own words.

## 4  Is your quotation exactly the same as the original or, if not, have you indicated what changes you have made?

### Indicating changes made to a quotation

- Use three spaced dots (ellipsis) if you leave anything out of a quotation.
- Use square brackets if you add to a quotation to make the meaning clear or to fit it grammatically into your own sentence.
- If your quotation already has a quotation within it, show this by giving the inside quotation different quotation marks (single or double) to the ones you have used for the main quotation.

Below is a text extract followed by an essay extract to show you the use of all four types of changes.

### Source extract:
Use of percentage GDA signals on front-of-pack labeling has been promoted by some sections of the food industry as an alternative to a 'traffic-light' signposting system …

Lobstein T, Landon, J and Lincoln P (2007) *Misconceptions and misinformation:The problems with Guideline Daily Amounts (GDAs).*

### Student essay
*Lobstein et al. (2007) state that 'use of percentage GDA [Guideline Daily Amounts] signals … has been promoted … as an alternative to a "traffic light" signposting system' (p1).*

## 5  Have you used the correct punctuation?

Use a *colon* in front of the quotation if you have used a complete sentence to introduce it.

Example:
> *Winterson uses the sea as a metaphor for life: 'Shoal of babies vied for life' (Lighthousekeeping, p3).*

Use a *comma* in front of the quotation if you have used a phrase to introduce it.

Example:

> *As Tomalin (2010) states, 'Pepys was …*
> *mapping a recognizably modern world' (p148).*

*Don't use any punctuation* if you integrate your quotation into the rest of your sentence.

Example:

> *Polkinghorne describes a quantum as 'a kind*
> *of little bullet' (Polkinghorne, 2002, p10).*

## 6  Have you acknowledged the source correctly?

You must always indicate where your quotation comes from, either by using a name/year referencing system (e.g. Harvard, APA, MLA) or a numeric system (e.g. Numeric British Standard). Importantly, in addition to acknowledging your sources in your writing, you must also give full details of your references in your bibliography or list of references at the end of your written text.

## 7  Have you used too many quotations?

The number of quotations you use will vary according to your discipline and assignment. As a very general rule, only use short quotations once or twice a page at most.

For more on how to use quotations, see *How to use your reading in your essays* pp30–6 and *Referencing and understanding plagiarism* Ch 6.

# using your own words: paraphrase and summary

Using your own words to re-express source material enables you to:

- express the information in your own style so that it fits into the rest of your writing
- restate the information in a way that supports your own argument
- restate information more clearly and simply
- find out for *yourself* whether or not you really understand your material
- show your *tutor* that you understand your material and that you also understand the position of different authors on the topic and how they relate to each other.

## Paraphrasing

You will sometimes want to re-express an idea contained in a short section of source material. This is referred to as paraphrasing.

Example:

### *Source extract*

One of the interesting facts about recent happiness research is how its empirical findings have been found to generalize across countries.

> Blanchflower DG and Oswald A (2011) 'International Happiness' Working Paper 16668, National Bureau of Economic Research.

### Student paraphrase

*Importantly, as Blanchflower and Oswald (2011) point out, research indicates that the factors that affect people's levels of happiness are universal.*

## Summarising

A more common reason for using your own words and style is to summarise a longer section of text or a whole text. Summaries can be short and powerful, often giving the main point of one or more texts in just a couple of sentences.

Example:

### A two-sentence summary that contrasts the position of two different sources

*One model of job satisfaction is based on the idea that jobs with particular characteristics attract people with particular personality attributes, which in turn affect how satisfied a person will be with their job (Oldham and Hackman, 1981). In contrast to this model, the dispositional approach sees a person's personality as the most important element in determining the level of job satisfaction, regardless of job type (Staw, Bell and Clausen 1986).*

## Steps for writing an effective paraphrase or summary:

1 Read, re-read, make notes and reflect on your material until you really understand and feel familiar with it.

2 When you make notes from source material, use some of your own words and phrases and make sure your notes record which phrases are copied down word for word (quotations), which are a mix of you and the source, and which are all you.

3 Write your paraphrase or summary from your memory and notes rather than by looking back at the original text.

4 For summaries, first try to encapsulate the whole text in just a sentence or two – you can go back and write a more detailed summary later if you want to.

5   Once you have integrated your paraphrase or
    summary into your writing, read it through and
    check that is supports the point you are making.
    Make clear to the reader the relevance of this
    source material to your own point.

> Attention! Using your own words does not make
> the *content or ideas* your own. You must therefore
> always reference paraphrases and summaries.

## How much do you need to change the original text?

Paraphrases and summaries are always assumed to
consist of nearly all your own words and sentence
patterns, and so a 'half and half' approach (half your
words and half theirs) is not acceptable. If you follow
the five steps above you will naturally use your own
words to re-express source material.

Below is a source extract followed by two student
paraphrases.

### Source extract

It is clearly best if the [stem] cells used in
transplantation can be taken from the patient him-
or herself, to avoid rejection by the body. While
embryonic cells have been proposed as a means of
avoiding rejection problems, even early embryonic
cells have surface molecules which can cause an
immune response.

> Jones D 2002. A Submission to The House of Lords
> Select Committee on Stem Cell Research.

For more on how to paraphrase, see *How to
use your reading in your essays* pp37–45 and
*Referencing and understanding plagiarism* Ch 6.

## Student paraphrase 1 ✗

Another key reason for moving research away from use of embryonic cells is that of tissue rejection. Jones (2002) points out that tissue used for transplanting <u>can be taken from patients</u> so that rejection does not occur. Cells from embryos <u>have been proposed as a means of avoiding rejection problems</u>, but even these <u>cells have surface molecules</u> that can create a response from the immune system.

Too many phrases from the original and this paraphrase has exactly the same information and sentence pattern as the original text.

## Student paraphrase 2 ✓

First sentence helps paraphrase flow smoothly into the essay and shows how it will support the student's own point.

Another key reason for moving research away from use of embryonic cells is that of tissue rejection. Jones (2002) points out that rejection problems do occur with cells taken from embryos due to the molecules on the cell surface, and that it is therefore better to use the patient's own cells for transplantation procedures.

Student's own words and style. All words changed except for 'embryonic cells', 'rejection' and 'molecular'.

Tips for rewriting the original
- Reverse the order of information.
- Use different sentence structures.
- Use synonyms, e.g. immune response → rejection problem.
- Use different word forms, e.g. embryonic cells → cells from embryos.

# showing that you understand what your sources are doing

### Use the right reporting verb for the job

Show that you understand exactly what an author is doing in the original text by using the right verb.

For example

*Lawton (2009) <u>describes</u> the different uses of pain relieving drugs.*

is very different from

*Lawton (2009) <u>questions</u> the different uses of pain relieving drugs.*

To help you choose the right verbs, ask yourself what the author is trying to *do* in different parts of their text and in the text overall. Are they putting forward an argument, reporting findings and implications, giving recommendations, offering solutions, or some of these things combined?

# making sure your own voice stands out

Your tutor will usually want to know what *you* consider to be most important about the topic or issue and why. Your 'written voice' will emerge through:

- clarity and soundness of your analysis, evaluation and conclusions (see Part 2)
- clear referencing to show which ideas are yours and which are from sources (see Parts 3 and 4)
- your choice and evaluation of sources and how you link sources to *your* points (see below).

## Show how your sources support your own points

Below are two versions of an essay paragraph. In extract A, the student paraphrases Robinson without showing why he does so. In version B, however, the student makes clear how Robinson is relevant to her own argument (these sections are underlined for your reference).

| Version A ✗ | Version B ✔ |
|---|---|
| *Robinson (2003:50) points out that whilst a bilingual speaker might understand two languages, a translator also has to be able to manipulate them.* | *As further support for my argument that you can't necessarily translate just because you can read a language,* *Robinson (2003:50) points out that whilst a bilingual speaker might understand two languages, a translator also has to be able to manipulate them.* *So, to be able to translate successfully requires more than just 'knowing the words' of the language.* |

## Use reporting verbs to show what you think about a source

Another important and powerful use for reporting verbs is to indicate your position in relation to the author/s. If you are going to agree with the author you can use a neutral or positive verb to report their idea. If you are going to disagree with the author, you shouldn't use a positive verb to do so.

   ✗ Example: *Tanen (2000) established that visual imprinting occurs in infancy. However, this was shown to be incorrect by later studies.*

| Positive verbs | Neutral verbs |
|---|---|
| confirm | argue |
| demonstrate | assert |
| describe | assume |
| establish | claim |
| find | conclude |
| illustrate | contend |
| note | maintain |
| observe | state |
| point out | suggest |
| show | |

# Other language for showing your position towards a source

| Indicating a positive position | Indicating a negative position |
| --- | --- |
| Smith's research … benefits from considers all aspects correctly identifies examines in great detail | Smith's research … fails to consider neglects the fact that overlooks suffers from wrongly assumes |
| Smith's research is … conclusive important interesting reliable sound valid | Smith's research is … flawed inconclusive limited questionable unreliable unsatisfactory |

## Show appropriate levels of caution

Be wary of expressing absolute certainty.

Examples:

   **✗** *The data proves the existence of automatic ageism.*

   **✗** *Removing speed cameras will result in an increase in the number of road deaths.*

Even though you think there is overwhelming evidence for something, someone else may think differently, and even the most eminent scientists have to accept that they might be wrong. We show this contestable nature of knowledge by using 'cautious' language such as *I suggest / This might indicate / This would seem to / appear to show …*

Using cautious language also helps persuade your reader rather than sounding as if you are telling them what to think.

For more on using reporting verbs and phrases in your writing, see *How to use your reading in your essays* pp65–93.

**7**

# having a clear and logical structure

## Use signposting language

'Structure signposts' help guide your reader through your work. However, don't use lots of signposting language to try and cover up a lack of good content or ideas in your writing. Do use signposts to make clear to your reader how your points connect, contrast and develop.

Examples of signposting language:

**Saying what you are going to do/order points**

In this essay I will / This essay will …

**Adding another similar point**

In addition / an additional x is / another x is

**Moving on to a contrasting point**

In contrast / by contrast / conversely

**Moving on to a different point**

As for / regarding / with regard to / moving on to / with respect to

**Restating/rephrasing**

In other words / that is to say / put another way / to put it more simply,

**Introducing alternative views**

An opposing view is / another possibility is / others argue that / it could also be argued that

### Showing cause/result

Because / since / therefore / thus / so as /
this means that / this results in / as a result /
consequently / the

### Concluding

To conclude, / in conclusion, / to summarise,

## Paragraph structure

The exact way you structure your writing will depend
on your particular writing context (a lab report will
have a very different structure to a discursive essay)
but many writing formats will require clear, well-
structured paragraphs.

Each paragraph should have a start, middle and
end and should focus on one idea. Each should
have a logical flow and the reader should be able
to see how the theme of the paragraph adds to or
contrasts with that of the previous one. At the end
of each paragraph your reader should feel that they
have read a manageable chunk of your assignment
and have reached an appropriate place to pause for
thought before reading on.

Below is an extended version of the essay paragraph
we looked at on p18 that is part of an essay
addressing the title: *Anyone who can read in
another language can translate it*. The paragraph
is annotated to show the structural and language
techniques used to give it a clear structure.

For more on paragraph structure, see *Planning your
essay* and *Brilliant writing tips for students*.

| Order of ideas | | Words and phrases used |
|---|---|---|
| **Start**<br><br>The paragraph starts by showing its relevance to the essay title and student's overall point and by making a link to the previous paragraph.<br><br>Gives the topic of the paragraph | As further support for my argument that you can't necessarily translate just because you can read a language, Robinson (2003:50) points out that whilst a bilingual speaker might understand two languages, a translator also has to be able to manipulate them. Such manipulation requires knowledge of the cultural and semantic meaning around and behind words, as well as what is on the page, together with an ability to translate even when there may not be direct word equivalents between the two languages – an idea explored in detail in | words and phrases that show the sequence and logical order of the ideas<br><br><br>repetition or near-repetition of key words that glue the paragraph content together |
| **Middle**<br><br>Explores the topic and integrates supporting evidence | Grosjean (1984). So, to be able to translate successfully requires more than just 'knowing the words' of the language. | |
| **End**<br><br>Summarises the point made | The study and training needed to become skilled in manipulating language as a translator is another factor … | |

# writing in a clear style

This mini-guide has already covered several aspects of academic writing that go towards the development of a clear writing style:

- using evidence and logic to develop a rigorous argument  pp5–7
- using source material correctly and effectively  pp8–15
- making sure your written voice is clear by using appropriate verbs and other phrases to report and show your evaluation of sources  pp17–19
- showing appropriate levels of caution  p19
- using logical content and clear signposting to give structure to your writing  pp20–22

The rest of this section will take you through the other aspects of language necessary for a clear writing style.

## Features of formality

Formal writing is not just speech written down – students sometimes lose marks because their writing is too much like everyday speech.

| Don't | Do |
|---|---|
| Use contractions – *it's/can't/won't* | Write using full word forms and sentences. Learn how to use punctuation correctly to help convey meaning. |
| Use word abbreviations e.g. *dept./gov. e.g./i.e.* | Use acronyms (e.g. NATO) accurately and give the full form with the acronym in brackets at the first mention. |
| Use vague 'run on' expressions – *etc., and so on, and so forth*: *A healthy lifestyle means eating well, exercising and so forth.* | Finish your sentence with precision: ... *exercising, a good work-life balance and a generally healthy environment.* |
| Use questions: *So, what are the main causes of global warming?* An occasional question for impact is okay but they can make your writing look informal. | Use indirect questions that have an introductory phrase and non-question word order: *The key question is what the main causes of global warming are.* |
| Address the reader as 'you' because this sounds as if you are giving them an order: *You need to think about possible solutions.* | Use 'we' or the passive form: *We need to think ... / Possible solutions need to be found.* |
| Use rude or emotional adjectives: *awful, ridiculous, stupid, pretty (very), lovely, terrible.* | Use evidence and argument to reach reasoned and objective judgements. |
| Use *stuff, thing.* | Use precise vocabulary: *theory, idea, action, issue.* |
| Use *a bit, a lot of, plenty of/huge.* | Use more formal vocabulary: *a small amount, much, a large amount of.* |
| Use the verb *get* or two-part verbs: *cut down, make up, got worse, brought up, set up, look into, put up with, find out.* | Find precise, formal equivalents for two-part verbs: *reduce, compensate, worsened, raised, established, investigate, tolerate, discover.* |

# Don't use speech-like phrases and clichés

These are informal and also vague and/or meaningless. It is better to explain things in your own words.

## Don't use . . .

| | |
|---|---|
| anyway, | to name but a few |
| basically, | easier said than done |
| at the end of the day, | that's another story |
| it all comes down to | to put it mildly |
| the thing is, | keep a lid on |
| along the way | leave no stone unturned |
| beyond a shadow of a | a different ball game |
| doubt | see the light at the end |
| in a nutshell | of the tunnel |
| last but not least | |

## Write powerful sentences

Academic writing tends to pack a lot of information into a small amount of text by using a high proportion of *noun phrases* rather than **wh-** or **subject + verb** phrases.

### Version A ✗ – less powerful

**The doctor will choose** which <u>drug to treat the patient with</u> depending on **whether he/she has had** previous health problems and on **what** they do for a living. If **they are someone who** is <u>resistant to penicillin,</u> **the doctor will** also need to do a skin test so that **they can check** for reactions that might cause problems.

### Version B ✔ – more powerful

<u>***The treatment drug***</u> depends on the ***patient's medical history*** and ***current occupation.*** <u>***Penicillin-resistant patients***</u> will also need a skin test to check for potential negative reactions.

Notice also that in version B the main point (underlined) is at the start of each sentence. Giving your main point at the start or end of a sentence is more powerful than burying it somewhere in the middle.

## Don't overuse abstract nouns

Don't overuse abstract nouns (nouns that end in
*-tion, -ism, -ness, -nce, -ity,* often followed by *of*). If
they are making a sentence clumsy and unclear, use
the verb/adjective form instead.

Example:
    The <u>organisation</u> of the compilation of the
    legislation was poor.  ✘
    The compilation of the legislation <u>was</u> poorly
    <u>organised.</u>  ✔

## Don't overuse the passive tense

You will sometimes need to use the passive tense
but the passive can make your sentence overly
complicated and weak. If this happens, use the
active tense instead or leave out the passive phrase
altogether.

| Overuse of passive | Active |
|---|---|
| It needs to be emphasized that this theory has several flaws. | This theory has several flaws. |
| It has been recommended by Government that schools require students to … | The Government has recommended that schools require students … |

## Strike the right balance of sentence length

It's good to have some short and some longer
sentences. What's important is to think about how
clear, flowing and powerful your sentences will be to
your reader. Avoid lots of sentences that have 35+
words or more than two *wh-* / *that-* / *if* / – *but* – /
*-ing* clauses and also avoid using a series of very
short sentences.

### One sentence – too long. ✘

In 2014, 46% of all adults released from UK prisons reoffended within a year, and this figure was even higher (58%) for adults who had finished a prison sentence of twelve months or less, and the figures are even higher for juveniles with nearly 70% of under-eighteens reoffended after release.[2]

### Four sentences – too many. ✘

In 2014, 46% of all adults released from UK prisons reoffended within a year. This figure was even higher (58%) for adults who had finished a prison sentence of twelve months or less. The figures are even higher for juveniles. Nearly 70% of under-eighteens reoffended after release.[2]

### Two sentences – okay. ✔

In 2014, 46% of all adults released from UK prisons reoffended within a year, and this figure was even higher (58%) for adults who had finished a prison sentence of twelve months or less**.**[1] The figures are even higher for juveniles with nearly 70% of under-eighteens reoffended after release.[2]

## Be succinct

Writing in a formal style and discussing complex ideas does *not* mean that you have to use as many 'long words' as possible (academic articles that do so are probably poorly written). Aim to convey complex ideas succinctly, avoiding words or phrases that are overly complicated:

*This essay will commence with* ✘ / *start with* ✔
*The tower was fabricated in* ✘ / *built in* ✔

or that merely repeat the previous word:

*absolutely essential* ✘ – *essential* ✔
*conclusive proof* ✘ – *proof* ✔
*close proximity* ✘ – *proximity* ✔
*different varieties* ✘ – *varieties* ✔
or, *alternatively* ✘ – *alternatively* ✔

## Be authentic

Don't copy someone else's style and don't use words you don't fully understand. Your tutor would rather see you explain your ideas clearly in less formal words than unclearly in more complicated language. If you can't write clearly about something it's probably because you don't yet understand it or haven't properly developed your ideas about it.

## Use words precisely

The main reason for using more formal vocabulary is that it is powerful and precise, enabling you to explain even complex ideas with brevity and accuracy. It is, however, all too easy to use a word incorrectly or in a 'nearly but not quite right' way.

Examples:

There are a ~~distinct~~ range of ethnic groups in London. (diverse)

Pollution from the new factories has ~~exaggerated~~ the problem. (exacerbated)

Polio vaccinations in the 1960s had virtually ~~prevented~~ the disease by the 1970s. (eliminated/eradicated)

Remember that it's not enough to know what a word means when you read it – you need to be able to *use* it accurately in your own writing. Develop an active vocabulary by using a good dictionary and practising using words that you think are useful.

---

For more on using academic vocabulary, see *How to use your reading in your essays* pp61–97 and *The student phrase book*.

## Linked books in the *Palgrave Study Skills* and *Pocket Study Skills* series

Copus J (2009). *Brilliant writing tips for students*. Basingstoke: Palgrave Macmillan.

Cottrell S (2011). *Critical thinking skills* (2nd edition). Basingstoke: Palgrave Macmillan.

Cottrell S (2013). *The study skills handbook* (4th edition). Basingstoke: Palgrave Macmillan.

Godfrey J (2013). *How to use your reading in your essays* (2nd edition). Basingstoke: Palgrave Macmillan.

Godfrey J (2014). *Reading and making notes* (2nd edition). Basingstoke: Palgrave Macmillan.

Godfrey J (2013). *The student phrase book*. Basingstoke: Palgrave Macmillan.

Godfrey J (2011). *Writing for university*. Basingstoke: Palgrave Macmillan.

Godwin J (2014). *Planning your essay* (2nd edition). Basingstoke: Palgrave Macmillan.

Greetham B (2013). *How to write better essays* (3rd edition). Basingstoke: Palgrave Macmillan.

Williams K (2014). *Getting critical* (2nd edition). Basingstoke: Palgrave Macmillan.

Williams K and Carroll J (2009). *Referencing and understanding plagiarism*. Basingstoke: Palgrave Macmillan.

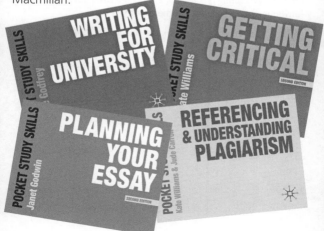

First published 2015 by
PALGRAVE

Palgrave in the UK is an imprint of Macmillan Publishers Limited, registered in England, company number 785998, of 4 Crinan Street, London, N1 9XW.

Palgrave Macmillan in the US is a division of St Martin's Press LLC, 175 Fifth Avenue, New York, NY 10010.

Palgrave is a global imprint of the above companies and is represented throughout the world.

Palgrave® and Macmillan® are registered trademarks in the United States, the United Kingdom, Europe and other countries.

ISBN: 978–1–137–54111–6 paperback

This book is printed on paper suitable for recycling and made from fully managed and sustained forest sources. Logging, pulping and manufacturing processes are expected to conform to the environmental regulations of the country of origin.

A catalogue record for this book is available from the British Library.

A catalog record for this book is available from the Library of Congress.